From Confucius to Code

Mastering Prompt Engineering on DeepSeek

EDWARD MORRIS

AS SEEN IN TIMES SQUARE, THE FINANCIAL TIMES, FORBES, AND MORE

Contents

1. Introduction to Prompt Engineering & DeepSeek

1.1 What is Prompt Engineering?

- Definition, importance, and real-world applications.
- Why mastering prompts enhances AI interactions.

1.2 Why DeepSeek?

- Overview of DeepSeek's features: Free access, R1 reasoning model, parity with GPT-4o.
- Unique strengths: Speed, accuracy, and adaptability for creative and analytical tasks.

---

2. Understanding LLMs and DeepSeek's Architecture

2.1 How LLMs Work (Simplified)

- Basics of tokenization, training data, and probabilistic text generation.

2.2 DeepSeek's R1 Model

- Focus on reasoning capabilities and how it compares to ChatGPT-4o.
- Key scenarios where DeepSeek excels (e.g., coding, logical problem-solving).

---

3. Core Principles of Effective Prompting

3.1 Clarity & Specificity

- Avoiding ambiguity; using explicit instructions.

3.2 Contextual Framing

- Providing background, role assignments (e.g., "Act as a physicist").

3.3 Iterative Refinement

- Testing, analyzing outputs, and adjusting prompts.

3.4 Balancing Openness vs. Constraints

- When to guide vs. let the model explore.

---

4. Prompting Techniques & Frameworks

4.1 Foundational Techniques

- Zero-shot, Few-shot, Chain-of-Thought prompting (examples included).

4.2 Advanced Frameworks

- **RACE Framework:** Role, Action, Context, Examples.
- **TAG Method:** Task, Audience, Goal.
- **STEP Approach:** Specify, Test, Evaluate, Polish.

4.3 Specialized Tactics for DeepSeek-R1

- Leveraging reasoning capabilities for puzzles, code, or data analysis.

---

5. Common Mistakes & Troubleshooting

5.1 Pitfalls to Avoid

- Vague prompts, overloading with context, ignoring model limitations.

5.2 Debugging Poor Outputs

- Strategies for rephrasing, simplifying, or adding examples.

5.3 When to Switch Techniques

- Recognizing when few-shot vs. chain-of-thought is more effective.

---

6. Advanced Prompt Engineering for Intermediates

6.1 Meta-Prompts

- Using DeepSeek to refine its own prompts (e.g., "Improve this prompt for clarity").

6.2 Recursive Prompting

- Breaking complex tasks into multi-step interactions.

6.3 Hybrid Prompts

- Combining creative and analytical tasks (e.g., "Write a poem explaining quantum physics").

---

7. Real-World Applications & Case Studies

7.1 Use Cases by Domain

- Coding, content creation, research, education, and business analytics.

7.2 Case Studies

- Example 1: Generating Python code with step-by-step debugging.
- Example 2: Writing a marketing campaign using RACE Framework.

---

8. Optimizing for DeepSeek's Unique Features

8.1 Maximizing R1's Reasoning Power

- Prompts for logic puzzles, mathematical proofs, or decision trees.

8.2 Cost-Free Efficiency

- Strategies for long-form content generation without API costs.

8.3 Customizing Output Formats

- Structuring prompts for JSON, markdown, or bullet-point responses.

---

9. Ethical Considerations

9.1 Bias Mitigation

- Crafting prompts to avoid harmful or biased outputs.

9.2 Transparency & Accountability

- Ensuring clarity about AI-generated content.

---

10. Tools & Resources

10.1 Prompt Libraries

- Curated repositories for DeepSeek-specific prompts.

10.2 Community & Support

- Forums, Discord groups, and DeepSeek documentation.

10.3 Automation Tools

- Browser extensions or templates for prompt management.

---

11. Conclusion & Next Steps

- Recap of key lessons.
- Encouragement to experiment and join communities.
- Future trends in prompt engineering.

Appendices (Bonus Stuff)

A. Cheat Sheet

- Quick-reference table of frameworks and techniques.

B. Glossary

- Definitions of key AI and prompt engineering terms.

C. FAQ

- Addressing common queries (e.g., "Why does DeepSeek sometimes ignore my constraints?").

D. Prompt Templates

- Fill-in-the-blank templates for various tasks.

Closing Thoughts

- The future of AI and Prompt Engineering.
- How to stay ahead and leverage AI as an asset.
- Final words on applying AI mastery to real-world problems.

Chapter 1: Introduction to Prompt Engineering & DeepSeek

1.1 What is Prompt Engineering?

Most people use AI like they use Google. They type in a question, hit enter, and pray the machine spits out something useful. **That's not Prompt Engineering. That's gambling.**

Prompt Engineering is the art and science of getting Large Language Models (or LLMs) to bend to your will. It's not magic, and it's not luck. It's **leverage**—knowing exactly what to say to extract the highest quality response from an AI like DeepSeek.

Think of it like training a world-class assistant. If you give vague, lazy instructions, you'll get vague, lazy results. If you structure your requests like a professional, you get professional output. AI is a high-performance engine, but if you treat it like a children's toy, you'll never go beyond basic outputs.

Why Prompt Engineering Matters

Right now, most people don't know how to talk to AI. That means you have a massive advantage if you do. Companies pay insane amounts of money for people who can consistently extract high-value outputs from LLMs. Why? Because most users **waste time fighting with AI instead of making it work for them.**

Good prompts can:

- Generate entire marketing campaigns in seconds.
- Solve complex coding problems faster than most developers.
- Break down difficult concepts like you're being taught by an elite professor.
- Act as a business consultant, strategist, and researcher all in one.

This isn't about writing *better prompts.* It's about **controlling AI like a weapon.** The better you prompt, the better your results, and the more leverage you have over people who don't understand this skill.

The Hidden Skill of the Future

A few years ago, nobody knew how valuable being a social media strategist would be. Then suddenly, brands started throwing money at people who could **go viral on**

command. The same thing is happening with Prompt Engineering.

Right now, there's a **gold rush** in AI, and the people who can craft high-quality prompts are the ones striking gold. Everyone else? They're just picking through the scraps, using AI at a fraction of its real power.

If you want to **automate work, gain leverage, and supercharge productivity**, mastering Prompt Engineering is the next step. This is the difference between people who **command** AI and those who get left behind.

1.2 Why DeepSeek?

DeepSeek is not just another AI. It's a **game-changer.**

Everyone's been obsessed with OpenAI's models (GPT-4o, GPT-4 Turbo) and Claude. But DeepSeek? It's one of the best-kept secrets in the AI world. **Free. Fast. Freakishly good at reasoning.**

What Makes DeepSeek Special?

- **GPT-4o Level Power** – This isn't some weak, undercooked chatbot. It's on par with the best models out there—except it doesn't cost you a cent.
- **R1 Model: Built for Reasoning** – DeepSeek's R1 architecture is **insanely good at logic-based**

tasks. It handles complex multi-step reasoning better than most other LLMs in its class. If you need structured outputs, step-by-step problem-solving, or AI that can **actually think through a problem**, R1 is your best friend.

- **Speed & Efficiency** – Most high-powered AI models come with **a catch**—either they're expensive or slow. DeepSeek is neither. It's free and fast, making it perfect for rapid iteration, business use, and on-the-fly experimentation.

Where DeepSeek Shines

Every LLM has strengths and weaknesses. DeepSeek isn't just a ChatGPT clone—it has some **clear advantages.**

🔥 **Reasoning & Logical Thinking** – Unlike some models that struggle with logical sequences, DeepSeek R1 can analyze, deduce, and respond in a way that actually makes sense. This makes it **perfect for coding, math, and structured decision-making.**

⚡ **Coding & Debugging** – Need an AI-powered dev assistant? DeepSeek excels at writing and debugging code. Unlike some models that hallucinate or make sloppy mistakes, DeepSeek follows logical structures **more reliably.**

⬛ **Data & Business Analytics** – If you know how to prompt it correctly, DeepSeek can break down complex datasets, analyze business trends, and provide insights that actually matter.

🧠 **Creativity & Long-Form Writing** – DeepSeek isn't just good at numbers. It's also great for content generation, storytelling, and crafting structured long-form pieces. If you give it the right guidance, it can write at a **near-human** level.

DeepSeek vs. The Competition

Let's be real—there are **a lot** of AI models out there. But let's compare DeepSeek with its biggest competitors:

Model	Strengths	Weaknesses
DeepSeek R1	Free, powerful reasoning, strong for logic-heavy tasks	Not as well-known, fewer integrations than OpenAI
GPT-4o	Strong general knowledge, great for natural conversation	Expensive, weaker at long logical chains
Claude 3+	Great memory, solid for long-term interactions	Can be slow, not as strong in coding

| Mistral | Open-source, great for fine-tuning | Requires more setup, lacks strong general reasoning |

The key takeaway? **DeepSeek punches way above its weight.** If you learn to use it effectively, you can achieve **GPT-4o-level results without paying a dime.**

Why This Guide Exists

Most Prompt Engineering guides are **boring, generic, and useless.** They recycle the same tips over and over: "Be clear," "Use examples," "Avoid ambiguity."

That's **not** what we're doing here.

This book is about **mastering the machine.** It's about controlling AI at a level most people never reach. You're going to learn:

- **Frameworks** that make your prompts 10x more effective.
- **Techniques** for advanced reasoning, creativity, and structured output.
- **Real-world applications** that you can use to make money, build businesses, or just level up your AI game.

This isn't theory. It's a **playbook.**

DeepSeek is one of the most powerful free tools available right now. If you know how to use it properly, you can outperform 99% of people who are blindly using AI like a glorified search engine.

Welcome to the **next level of AI mastery.**

Buckle up. We're just getting started.

Chapter 2: Understanding LLMs and DeepSeek's Architecture

2.1 How LLMs Work (Simplified)

Most people treat AI like a mystical oracle—something that "just works" without understanding what's actually happening behind the curtain. That's a mistake. If you don't understand how an LLM thinks, you'll never be able to manipulate it effectively.

So let's break it down.

The Basics of LLMs: A Controlled Chaos Machine

At its core, a Large Language Model (LLM) like DeepSeek isn't "thinking" in the way humans do. It's a **massive probability engine**. Every word it generates is calculated based on the statistical likelihood of what should come next.

Imagine playing a game of autocomplete on steroids. If you type, **"The capital of France is…"**, the model doesn't *know* Paris like you do—it just has an incredibly high probability that "Paris" is the correct next word.

Tokenization: How AI Sees Language

Before an LLM even *thinks* about generating text, it **breaks everything down into tokens**—which are basically bite-sized chunks of language. These tokens might be entire words (*dog*), subwords (*un-happy*), or even single letters in some cases.

For example, the sentence:

"DeepSeek is an insanely good AI."

Might be tokenized as:

```
[Deep] [Seek] [is] [an]
[insanely] [good] [AI] [.]
```

Each token is then fed into the model, which processes it using layers of artificial neurons that predict what comes next. The deeper the model, the more complex the calculations become, allowing it to generate **coherent, context-aware responses.**

The Training Process: How LLMs Become "Smart"

Training an LLM is **like feeding a machine the entire internet** (minus the garbage—hopefully). During training, DeepSeek learned patterns, grammar, facts, and reasoning by analyzing billions of text sources. This is called **pretraining.**

But here's the catch: **LLMs don't "think."** They just pattern-match at an absurdly high level.

That's why DeepSeek can write poetry, generate business strategies, and debug code, but it can also confidently **hallucinate** (i.e., make things up). Understanding this is key. You're not talking to an omniscient AI—you're talking to an ultra-intelligent parrot that knows how to sound convincing.

Fine-Tuning and RLHF: The Secret Sauce

After pretraining, DeepSeek was fine-tuned using **Reinforcement Learning from Human Feedback (RLHF)**—a fancy way of saying, "Humans corrected its mistakes until it got better."

This process helps curb bias, improve factual accuracy, and make responses **more useful and aligned with human expectations.** But it's not perfect, which is why **strong prompting techniques are still necessary** to guide it in the right direction.

2.2 DeepSeek's R1 Model: A Reasoning Powerhouse

Now that you understand how LLMs work, let's talk about what makes DeepSeek **special.**

The Power of the R1 Model

Most AI models struggle with multi-step reasoning. They can write a blog post or summarize an article just fine, but the moment you ask them to break down a complex problem step by step, they start tripping over themselves.

DeepSeek's R1 model is built differently. It **excels at structured reasoning, logical analysis, and systematic problem-solving.** This makes it a powerhouse for:

✔ **Coding & Debugging** – R1 can break down problems, explain solutions, and even suggest optimizations.

✔ **Mathematical & Logical Reasoning** – Unlike some LLMs that fumble through multi-step calculations, R1 follows structured logic exceptionally well.

✔ **Decision-Making & Planning** – Business analysis, strategy planning, and structured decision frameworks are where DeepSeek thrives.

How DeepSeek Compares to GPT-4o and Other Models

DeepSeek isn't trying to be a copy-paste version of ChatGPT. It has its own strengths. Let's compare:

Feature	DeepSeek R1	GPT-4o	Claude 3+	Mistral
Logical Reasoning	■ Strong	■ Strong	▲ Decent	▲ Moderate
Creativity & Storytelling	■ Good	■ Great	■ Excellent	▲ Moderate
Coding & Debugging	■ Strong	▲ Good	▲ Decent	■ Strong
Multi-Step Problem Solving	■ Excellent	▲ Good	▲ Moderate	▲ Decent
Free Access	■ Yes	▲ Sorta	▲ Sorta	▲ Sorta

Sorta? Why sorta? Because for accessing any of the other three, you need an upfront payment to continue using it.

Why This Matters for You

DeepSeek is **the perfect AI for structured tasks.** If you need an AI that can:

- Think through problems in a logical, step-by-step manner
- Generate structured outputs (e.g., code, business plans, research reports)
- Work **without** costly API fees

…then **DeepSeek is your secret weapon.**

The Takeaway: Understanding AI = Unlocking Power

Here's what you need to remember:

1. **AI is a probability machine.** It doesn't "think" like a human, but it can **mimic high-level reasoning patterns** if prompted correctly.
2. **DeepSeek's R1 model is built for reasoning.** While other models focus on general conversation, R1 thrives in logic-heavy tasks.
3. **Mastering AI starts with understanding how it works.** The more you grasp the mechanics, the better you can manipulate outputs to get exactly what you need.

Most people using AI are **casuals.** They throw in a random question and hope for a useful answer. But now, you **know how the machine thinks.** That's a level of control most people will never have.

Next Up: Core Principles of Effective Prompting

Now that you understand DeepSeek's strengths, the next step is learning **how to control it.** In the next chapter, we'll break down the **key principles** of crafting effective prompts—so you can start leveraging DeepSeek like a pro.

Let's get tactical. Time to **engineer your first high-performance prompts.**

Chapter 3: Core Principles of Effective Prompting

3.1 Clarity & Specificity: The Non-Negotiables

You wouldn't give an assistant half-baked instructions and expect perfection, right? So why do people treat AI that way?

When prompting DeepSeek (or any LLM), **clarity and specificity are non-negotiable.** If you're vague, you get vague. If you're clear, you get precision. It's that simple.

The Biggest Mistake People Make

Most users assume AI can "fill in the blanks" with common sense. That's wrong. LLMs predict based on probability, not true understanding. This means if you leave room for misinterpretation, **you will get inconsistent or inaccurate results.**

Example of a Bad Prompt:

"Tell me about marketing."

✗ What's wrong?

- Too broad. Are you asking about digital marketing, guerrilla marketing, or the psychology of consumer behavior?
- No target audience. Are you a beginner or a seasoned marketer?
- No desired output. Do you want an essay, bullet points, or a tweet-length summary?

Example of a Strong Prompt:

"Explain the fundamentals of digital marketing in a way that a small business owner with no prior experience can understand. Structure the response into three sections: (1) What digital marketing is, (2) Why it matters, and (3) Three beginner-friendly strategies they can implement right away."

■ What's right?

- **Specific request** – Digital marketing, not marketing in general.
- **Defined audience** – A small business owner with no prior experience.

- **Structured output** – Ensures the AI organizes the response logically.

Takeaway: Be explicit in what you want, how you want it, and who the response is for. The more you control the input, the more you control the output.

3.2 Contextual Framing: Teaching the AI How to Think

LLMs don't actually "think"—they pattern-match at an insanely high level. This means if you want DeepSeek to behave in a specific way, you need to frame the context properly.

Role Assignments: The Secret Weapon

One of the easiest ways to improve AI outputs is to assign it a role. This helps shape its response **by giving it a persona to work from.**

Example:

🚫 **Weak Prompt:** "Explain blockchain."

⬛ **Strong Prompt:** "You are a financial analyst who specializes in emerging technologies. Explain blockchain as if you are presenting it to executives who have no technical background."

🚀 **Next Level Prompt:** "You are a financial analyst who specializes in emerging technologies. Explain blockchain to a group of Fortune 500 executives who are considering investing in blockchain-related startups. Focus on the business applications and risks, avoiding unnecessary technical jargon."

See what happened? The AI is no longer just explaining blockchain—it's crafting a **tailored response** for a specific audience.

Setting Context for Multi-Turn Conversations

If you're engaging in a back-and-forth with DeepSeek, **maintain context between responses** by reiterating key details.

Example:

> **User:** "You are a business consultant. My company sells organic skincare products online, and we want to improve our conversion rates. What are three strategies we should try?"
>
> **DeepSeek:** [Gives three strategies]

User: "Great. Now, assuming our target audience is mostly women aged 25-40 who prioritize eco-friendly products, how would you refine these strategies?"

By re-establishing details in the follow-up, you help the AI **stay focused on your specific scenario.**

Takeaway: AI responds better when you define its "role" and reinforce contextual details. This leads to **more accurate and useful outputs.**

3.3 Iterative Refinement: Fine-Tuning Your Output

Most people stop after the first response. **That's a rookie mistake.**

AI is not a one-shot tool—it's a dialogue. The best results often come from iterating and refining.

The Three-Step Iteration Process

1. **Get the First Output:** Start with your initial prompt.
2. **Analyze & Identify Weaknesses:** Ask yourself, *Is this response clear? Does it match what I expected?*

3. **Refine the Prompt & Iterate:** Adjust your prompt and try again until you get the desired result.

Example:

⊘ **First Prompt:** "Write a social media caption for a new fitness app."

🤖 **AI Output:** "Check out our new fitness app! Stay fit, stay healthy!"

⬤ *Meh. Too generic.*

⬛ **Refined Prompt:** "Write a high-energy social media caption for Instagram that promotes a new fitness app. The caption should be short, engaging, and include a call to action."

🤖 **New AI Output:** "🔥 Get fit from anywhere! Download the ultimate fitness app now and crush your goals. 💪 #FitnessMadeEasy"

💯 *Much better.*

Takeaway: AI is **a tool, not a genie.** If the response isn't right, tweak the prompt and try again.

3.4 Balancing Openness vs. Constraints

There's a fine line between giving the AI **too much freedom** and **over-constraining it.**

If your prompt is too open-ended, the AI may **drift away from what you need.** If it's too restrictive, you might miss out on creative or insightful responses.

When to Guide vs. Let the AI Explore

+ **Use Constraints for Precision** – When you need a specific format, level of detail, or tone, provide constraints.

+ **Leave Room for Exploration** – When you want creative solutions, let the AI have some freedom.

Example:

⊘ **Overly Open Prompt:** "Give me business ideas."

■ **Balanced Prompt:** "Give me five business ideas in the health & wellness industry that require low startup costs."

⊘ **Overly Constrained Prompt:** "Give me one business idea for a yoga studio in downtown LA that only caters to professionals aged 30-35 and generates at least $500K in revenue."

Balanced Version: "Give me a business idea for a yoga studio in downtown LA. Focus on a niche audience and a revenue model that could generate six figures annually."

Takeaway: Find the sweet spot. **Guide the AI, but don't strangle its creativity.**

Final Thoughts: Mastering the Fundamentals

These four principles—Clarity, Context, Iteration, and Balance—are the foundation of great Prompt Engineering. Most AI users fumble around with bad prompts and wonder why they get mediocre results. **Now you know better.**

Next up: **Advanced Prompting Techniques & Frameworks**—where we take this skill from *good* to *unstoppable.*

Chapter 4: Prompting Techniques & Frameworks

4.1 Foundational Techniques: Zero-shot, Few-shot, and Chain-of-Thought Prompting

At this point, you understand the **fundamentals**—clarity, context, iteration, and balancing constraints. Now, we get tactical. We move from **theory to execution.**

The best prompters don't "wing it." They use **structured techniques** to get high-quality outputs **every time.**

Zero-Shot Prompting: The Baseline

Zero-shot prompting is what **most people do by default**—giving an LLM a prompt **without examples** and expecting it to perform well.

🚫 Bad Zero-Shot Prompt:

> "Explain SEO."

■ Better Zero-Shot Prompt:

"Explain SEO in simple terms, as if you're talking to a beginner who owns a small online business. Provide three actionable tips they can implement today."

When to Use Zero-Shot Prompting

- When the task is **simple or well-defined** (e.g., definitions, summaries, fact-based responses).
- When speed **matters more than precision.**
- When you **don't have good examples** to provide.

Zero-shot works **sometimes,** but if you want **precision and nuance,** you'll need to level up.

Few-Shot Prompting: Guiding the AI with Examples

Few-shot prompting **adds examples** to guide the AI toward a specific kind of response.

⊘ Basic Prompt:

"Write a social media post for a coffee shop."

🤖 **(AI might return something generic)**: *"Come get the best coffee in town! ☕"*

⚫ *Too basic. We can do better.*

⬛ **Few-Shot Prompt with Examples:**

> "Write a social media post for a coffee shop. Here are three examples of posts we liked:
>
> ☐1 'Nothing beats the smell of fresh-brewed espresso on a Monday morning. ☕ Come grab yours today! #MondayMotivation'
>
> ☐2 'Your morning coffee is waiting. ☀ Start the day with something delicious—our baristas have your back. #CoffeeLover'
>
> ☐3 'Fuel your day with the perfect blend. What's your go-to coffee order? Drop it in the comments! 👇 #CaffeineFix'
>
> Now, generate a similar post with a friendly, engaging tone."

🔥 **Few-shot works because it:**

- Gives **concrete examples** of what you want.
- Ensures consistency in **tone, structure, and quality.**
- Reduces **random, unpredictable outputs.**

When to Use Few-Shot Prompting

- When you need **a specific style, format, or structure.**
- When the AI struggles to stay **consistent.**
- When the **task is complex or creative.**

Chain-of-Thought Prompting: Teaching the AI to Think Step-by-Step

Most LLMs struggle with **multi-step reasoning.** If you don't structure your prompts correctly, they might **jump to conclusions** or skip important steps.

Chain-of-Thought (CoT) prompting **forces the AI to think in structured steps.**

⊘ **Bad Prompt:**

> "Solve this math problem: A store sells apples for $2 each. If you buy 5 apples and pay with a $20 bill, how much change do you get?"

🤖 **AI might rush to answer:** *"$10"* (wrong!).

◼ **CoT Prompt:**

> "Solve this math problem step-by-step: A store sells apples for $2 each. If you buy 5

apples and pay with a $20 bill, how much change do you get? Show your reasoning clearly."

AI's response:

1. The cost of one apple is $2.
2. The cost of 5 apples is 5 × $2 = $10.
3. The customer pays with a $20 bill.
4. The change is $20 - $10 = **$10.**

Correct answer with clear reasoning!

CoT works because it:

- Helps with **math, logic, and multi-step analysis.**
- Ensures the AI **explains its thought process.**
- Reduces **hallucinations and careless errors.**

When to Use Chain-of-Thought Prompting

- When the task requires **reasoning or logic.**
- When the AI **tends to jump to conclusions.**
- When you need an answer **with full step-by-step explanations.**

4.2 Advanced Frameworks for High-Performance Prompting

Now, let's talk **advanced prompting frameworks.** These are structured methods that let you consistently get **high-quality results.**

The RACE Framework: Role, Action, Context, Examples

RACE helps you create **clear, structured prompts** that minimize ambiguity.

■ **Example Prompt Using RACE:**

> **R**ole: You are a financial analyst.
>
> **A**ction: Write a report on the latest stock market trends.
>
> **C**ontext: Focus on tech stocks and explain whether they are overvalued.
>
> **E**xamples: Use recent data and reference major tech companies like Apple, Google, and Amazon.

The TAG Method: Task, Audience, Goal

TAG keeps prompts **focused and relevant.**

■ Example Prompt Using TAG:

Task: Summarize a complex scientific article.

Audience: High school students with no prior knowledge.

Goal: Make the summary engaging and easy to understand, using analogies where possible.

The STEP Approach: Specify, Test, Evaluate, Polish

STEP ensures that your prompts are **iterative and refined over time.**

■ Example:

Specify: Generate a persuasive email for a startup pitching investors.

Test: Run it and see if the tone is convincing.

Evaluate: Does it clearly communicate the company's value proposition?

Polish: Adjust wording and structure for maximum impact.

4.3 Specialized Tactics for DeepSeek-R1

Because DeepSeek is **built for reasoning,** you can optimize your prompts to maximize its strengths.

DeepSeek-Specific Prompting Tricks

1️⃣**Logic-Heavy Tasks:** Use **CoT prompting** for best results.
2️⃣**Coding & Debugging:** Provide **structured examples** and use **few-shot prompting.**
3️⃣**Complex Analysis:** Break down tasks into **step-by-step instructions.**
4️⃣**Creative Writing:** Use **RACE or TAG** to shape the style and audience.

🔥 **DeepSeek is powerful, but only if you prompt it correctly.**

Final Thoughts: The Next-Level Prompter

By now, you should see that **prompting is an art AND a science.**

1. **Zero-shot works, but it's basic.**
2. **Few-shot gives better control.**
3. **Chain-of-Thought makes AI "think."**
4. **Frameworks like RACE, TAG, and STEP refine the process.**

Most people use AI like a **fisherman casting a wide net, hoping to catch something useful.** But you? You're now a sniper—**firing precise, high-impact prompts that get exactly what you need.**

Next up: **Common Mistakes & Troubleshooting.** Because even the best prompters hit roadblocks—and knowing how to fix them is what separates the amateurs from the pros.

Chapter 5: Common Mistakes & Troubleshooting

5.1 Pitfalls to Avoid: Why Your Prompts Are Failing

Even with all the techniques and frameworks you've learned so far, **bad prompts still happen**—and bad prompts lead to bad outputs. The difference between an amateur and an expert isn't that the expert never fails; it's that they **immediately know why a response went wrong and how to fix it.**

Here are the **most common mistakes** in Prompt Engineering—and how to avoid them.

1. Being Too Vague

🚫 **Bad Prompt:** "Tell me about AI."

🤖 *DeepSeek spits out a generic answer that doesn't help anyone.*

⬛ **Fix:** Be specific about what aspect of AI you want to explore.

✔ **Better Prompt:** "Explain AI in the context of financial trading. Focus on algorithmic strategies and risk management."

2. Overloading the Prompt with Too Much Context

🚫 **Bad Prompt:**

> "I need a summary of blockchain technology, but also explain how Bitcoin mining works, how Ethereum smart contracts function, and include a comparison between proof-of-work and proof-of-stake models. Also, can you write this as if I'm a 10-year-old but also in a professional tone?"

🤖 *DeepSeek gets confused and returns an unfocused mess.*

⬛ **Fix:** Break it down into multiple, clear prompts.

✔ **Better Prompt:**

> 1️⃣ "Explain blockchain technology in simple terms."
> 2️⃣ "Now, describe how Bitcoin mining works."
> 3️⃣ "Next, compare proof-of-work and proof-of-stake models."

3. Ignoring Model Limitations

🚫 **Bad Prompt:** "Write me a completely new, 500-page novel in the style of J.K. Rowling."

🤖 *DeepSeek might return a few paragraphs and then stop.*

⬛ **Fix:** Understand the model's constraints and work within them.

✔ **Better Prompt:** "Write a detailed plot outline for a fantasy novel in the style of J.K. Rowling."

4. Expecting Perfection on the First Try

🚫 **Bad Approach:** Getting frustrated when DeepSeek doesn't immediately give the perfect response.

⬛ **Fix:** Treat AI like an **iterative process.**

✔ **Better Approach:**

1. Run an initial prompt.
2. Analyze what's missing.
3. Adjust and refine.

5.2 Debugging Poor Outputs: Fixing AI Mistakes Fast

Even if you avoid common pitfalls, **LLMs can still produce garbage.** Knowing how to troubleshoot bad responses is a core skill for any Prompt Engineer.

1. The AI Output Is Too Generic

⊘ **Problem:** The response is vague, surface-level, and lacks insight.

■ **Solution:** Add constraints like depth, examples, and style.

✔ **Fix:** Instead of *"Explain digital marketing"*, try:

> "Explain digital marketing for a startup with a limited budget. Provide three actionable strategies and real-world examples."

2. The AI Misunderstood the Question

⊘ **Problem:** The response is irrelevant or goes in the wrong direction.

■ **Solution:** Clarify the task or reframe the question.

✔ **Fix:** Instead of *"Describe inflation"*, try:

> "Describe inflation in the context of the 2008 financial crisis and its impact on real estate."

3. The AI Hallucinates Information

🚫 **Problem:** The response includes **wrong or made-up** facts.

⬛ **Solution:** Ask for **sources, citations, or reasoning.**

✔ **Fix:** Instead of *"What are the top scientific discoveries of 2024?"*, try:

> "List the top scientific discoveries of 2024 and cite reliable sources for each."

4. The AI Stops Mid-Sentence

🚫 **Problem:** The response gets cut off.

⬛ **Solution:** Tell the AI **to continue.**

✔ **Fix:** Use *"Continue from where you left off."* or *"Expand on the last point in more detail."*

5.3 When to Switch Techniques: Knowing What Works Best

If an AI isn't producing the right results, sometimes it's not the AI—it's your technique. Knowing **when to switch prompting strategies** is what separates casual users from Prompt Engineers.

1. When Zero-Shot Isn't Enough, Use Few-Shot

If DeepSeek struggles with creativity or nuance, give it examples.

🚫 **Bad Prompt:** "Write a product description for a fitness app."

⬛ **Fix:** Use a few-shot approach.

✔ **Better Prompt:**

> "Write a product description for a fitness app. Here are two examples of descriptions we like: [Insert Example 1] & [Insert Example 2]. Now, write something in a similar style."

---

2. When Outputs Lack Depth, Use Chain-of-Thought

If the response is too shallow, force the AI to **think in steps.**

🚫 **Bad Prompt:** "Explain how to start a business."

⬛ **Fix:** Use **Chain-of-Thought prompting.**

✔ **Better Prompt:**

> "Explain how to start a business step-by-step, covering ideation, validation, funding, and scaling. Provide real-world examples for each step."

---

3. When Creativity Is Needed, Use Role Assignments

If the AI's output feels **bland**, assign it a role.

🚫 **Bad Prompt:** "Write a blog post about AI."

⬛ **Fix:** Assign a role and audience.

✔ **Better Prompt:**

> "You are a tech journalist writing for Wired Magazine. Write a compelling article about the future of AI in healthcare, with expert analysis and industry trends."

Final Thoughts: Mastering AI Debugging

Most people get **one bad response and quit.** But now, you understand how to troubleshoot, refine, and adapt.

The **real skill in Prompt Engineering** isn't just knowing how to write prompts—it's knowing **how to fix bad ones.**

🔥 **Recap of Key Fixes:**

- **Be specific.** Remove vagueness.
- **Break down complex prompts.** Avoid overload.
- **Use iterations.** Don't expect perfection on the first try.
- **Adjust techniques.** Use Few-Shot, CoT, and Role Assignments when needed.

Next up: **Advanced Prompt Engineering for Intermediates.** Now that you can troubleshoot, it's time to go beyond basics and into **meta-prompting, recursive strategies, and hybrid techniques.** Buckle up—this is where things get crazy.

Chapter 6: Advanced Prompt Engineering for Intermediates

By now, you understand the core principles of effective prompting. You've learned how to be clear, how to frame context, how to iterate, and how to troubleshoot. But this is where we take things to the **next level.**

This chapter is about **advanced techniques**—the kind of methods that separate casual users from expert-level prompters who consistently generate **high-quality, structured, and optimized outputs.**

If you've ever felt like AI responses are "good, but not great," **this chapter fixes that.**

6.1 Meta-Prompts: Using AI to Optimize Its Own Prompts

The easiest way to improve your prompts? **Use AI to refine them.**

Instead of struggling to write the perfect prompt from scratch, let DeepSeek optimize it for you.

Example 1: Prompt Optimization

🚫 Basic Prompt:

"Write a blog post about AI in education."

⬛ Better Prompt Using AI:

"Improve this prompt: 'Write a blog post about AI in education.' Make it more specific, structured, and engaging."

🤖 DeepSeek's Response:

"Rewrite the prompt as: 'Write a 1,000-word blog post on the impact of AI in education. Focus on personalized learning, automation, and accessibility. Provide real-world examples and include expert insights.'"

Boom. **Instant improvement.**

Example 2: Refining Output Style

🚫 **Problem:** AI's tone doesn't match your needs.

⬛ **Fix:** Use meta-prompting to adjust the style.

✔ **Prompt:**

> "Rewrite the following response in a more engaging, conversational tone: [insert AI-generated text]."

Meta-prompts **supercharge your prompting workflow** by letting the AI fine-tune itself. **Don't do extra work if AI can do it for you.**

6.2 Recursive Prompting: AI That Thinks in Steps

Recursive prompting is the **art of breaking down complex tasks** into a multi-step process. Instead of expecting a **single, perfect** answer, you build up the response **iteratively.**

Example: Writing a Business Plan

🚫 Bad Prompt:

> "Write a business plan for an online fitness coaching startup."

🔩 *AI might generate a decent plan, but it'll probably be generic and lack depth.*

⬛ Recursive Fix:

1️⃣ "Generate a one-sentence mission statement for an online fitness coaching startup."

2️⃣ "Expand this into a full business vision statement."

3️⃣ "Now, outline a business model with revenue streams and customer acquisition strategies."

4️⃣ "Write an executive summary that summarizes everything concisely."

Each step **builds on the last,** making the final output **far stronger** than a single-shot attempt.

Recursive prompting is especially useful for:

- **Writing long-form content** (blog posts, whitepapers, reports).
- **Business strategy** (market analysis, financial planning, SWOT analysis).
- **Coding projects** (debugging, refactoring, optimizing code step-by-step).

6.3 Hybrid Prompts: Combining Creativity & Analysis

Most people assume prompts should be **either creative or analytical**—but the real magic happens when you **blend both.**

Example: A Scientific Poem

🚫 Standard Prompt:

"Write a poem about quantum mechanics."

💣 *AI might generate something poetic, but scientifically inaccurate.*

⬛ Hybrid Fix:

"Write a poem that explains quantum mechanics using accurate scientific terminology. The style should be similar to Robert Frost's poetry, making complex ideas feel simple and beautiful."

Example: A Data-Driven Story

🚫 Bad Prompt:

"Write a fictional story about a tech startup."

⬛ Better Hybrid Prompt:

"Write a fictional short story about a struggling tech startup. Use real startup failure statistics and reference actual tech industry trends to make it feel authentic."

By blending **creativity with hard facts,** you get **more engaging, high-quality outputs.**

6.4 Multi-Agent Prompting: Making AI Work as a Team

A single AI response isn't always enough. Sometimes, you need **multiple perspectives**—which is where multi-agent prompting comes in.

Instead of using just one prompt, you set up **multiple 'AI agents'** to interact with each other.

Example: Debate Between Experts

⊘ Basic Prompt:

"Explain the pros and cons of remote work."

■ Multi-Agent Fix:

"Imagine a debate between a tech CEO who supports remote work and an economist who argues against it. Write their conversation, making sure each presents strong, well-reasoned arguments."

🤖 *Now AI generates a back-and-forth discussion, making the response **far more engaging and nuanced.***

This technique is useful for:

- **Exploring multiple viewpoints** (debates, case studies, industry analysis).
- **Testing ideas before implementation** (business strategies, product design).
- **Creative brainstorming** (writing dialogues, simulating customer feedback).

6.5 Advanced Formatting & Output Structuring

Most AI users take whatever response they get and **manually clean it up.** Don't be like most AI users. **Structure your output upfront.**

Example: JSON Output for Automation

🚫 **Messy Prompt:**

> "List five books about AI."

🤖 *AI returns a simple list.*

⬛ **Optimized Prompt:**

"List five books about AI. Format the response in JSON with the following fields: title, author, publication year, and a one-sentence summary."

🤖 *Now AI generates something that can be directly plugged into an app or database.*

Example: Markdown for Readability

🚫 Unstructured Prompt:

"Summarize the latest AI research paper."

⬛ Formatted Fix:

"Summarize the latest AI research paper in a Markdown format. Use bullet points for key findings, bold headings for sections, and include a 'Key Takeaways' section at the end."

🤖 *Now you get a well-structured, readable response—ready for publishing.*

By **controlling the format upfront,** you eliminate wasted time **manually fixing** AI outputs.

Final Thoughts: Unlocking True AI Mastery

At this stage, you're **not just writing prompts—you're engineering them.**

🚀 **Key Takeaways from Chapter 6:**

1. **Meta-prompts let AI optimize itself**—use them to refine structure and style.
2. **Recursive prompting breaks down big tasks**—improving accuracy and depth.
3. **Hybrid prompts mix creativity & analysis**—leading to unique, engaging results.
4. **Multi-agent techniques create richer outputs**—perfect for debates, roleplays, and strategy planning.
5. **Advanced formatting saves time**—control output structure with JSON, Markdown, or bullet points.

Most people use AI at **surface level.** Now, you're operating at **a level most users never reach.**

Next Up: Real-World Applications & Case Studies

Now that you have advanced techniques, let's apply them to **real-world problems.** The next chapter will cover actual case studies—so you can see how everything comes together in high-impact AI workflows.

Chapter 7: Real-World Applications & Case Studies

Now that you've mastered the techniques of prompt engineering, it's time to put everything into action. **Theory is great, but execution is everything.**

This chapter will cover real-world applications and case studies that demonstrate how DeepSeek can be used **in practical, high-impact ways.** You'll see how experts use AI to solve problems, streamline workflows, and **create actual business value.**

7.1 Use Cases by Domain

1. Coding & Debugging

DeepSeek is a **powerful programming assistant**, capable of:

- Generating clean, optimized code from scratch.
- Debugging complex issues by explaining errors step by step.

- Refactoring messy code for efficiency and readability.
- Writing unit tests automatically to catch edge cases.

Real-World Example:

🚀 **Problem:** A startup needs an automated script to pull financial data from multiple APIs, but their developers are struggling to optimize the code.

⬛ **Solution:**

> "Analyze the following Python script for efficiency issues. Suggest optimizations and rewrite the script using best practices."

🤖 **AI Output:** DeepSeek not only optimizes the script but also explains why certain changes improve performance, making it an instant coding mentor.

---

2. Content Creation & Marketing

AI is revolutionizing content marketing. DeepSeek can:

- Generate blog posts, social media content, and ad copy.
- Optimize content for SEO and engagement.
- Create persuasive product descriptions and sales emails.

Real-World Example:

■ **Problem:** A digital agency wants to launch a viral social media campaign but lacks a strong hook.

■ **Solution:**

> "Create five engaging Twitter threads about the impact of AI on business. Each thread should start with a compelling hook and end with a strong CTA."

🤖 **AI Output:** DeepSeek generates structured, engaging threads that capture audience attention, complete with data-driven insights and persuasive messaging.

---

3. Research & Analysis

DeepSeek excels at breaking down **complex topics into digestible insights.**

- Summarizing lengthy research papers.
- Extracting key trends from industry reports.
- Providing structured comparisons between competing technologies or strategies.

Real-World Example:

🔬 **Problem:** A VC firm needs a rapid but **accurate** summary of the latest AI research to inform investment decisions.

⬛ **Solution:**

> "Summarize the key takeaways from the latest AI research paper on reinforcement learning. Provide a breakdown of its practical applications."

🏭 **AI Output:** DeepSeek condenses the paper into clear insights, **saving hours of manual research.**

---

4. Business Strategy & Decision-Making

CEOs, analysts, and consultants use AI to **augment their decision-making** by:

- Running SWOT analyses on business opportunities.
- Forecasting trends based on historical data.
- Generating investment theses and market research reports.

Real-World Example:

💡 **Problem:** A founder is unsure whether to pivot their startup's business model.

■ Solution:

> "Conduct a SWOT analysis of shifting from
> a SaaS model to a marketplace model.
> Provide key risks, advantages, and
> real-world examples."

▲ AI Output: DeepSeek generates a structured analysis, helping the founder **weigh the pros and cons** before making a critical decision.

7.2 Case Studies

Case Study 1: Automating a Legal Document Review Process

Company: Mid-sized law firm

Problem: Lawyers were spending 20+ hours per week reviewing contracts for compliance, leading to **wasted billable hours** and increased operational costs.

AI Solution:

> "Analyze this legal contract and identify any
> clauses that may be non-compliant with
> GDPR regulations."

Results:

- AI identified potential compliance issues in **minutes** instead of hours.
- Reduced **human error** by providing a checklist of risky clauses.
- Saved the firm **$15,000/month** in billable time.

🔥 **Key Takeaway: AI doesn't replace lawyers, but it makes them exponentially more efficient.**

Case Study 2: Enhancing E-Commerce Conversions with AI-Powered Chatbots

Company: Direct-to-consumer (DTC) skincare brand

Problem: Customer support was overwhelmed with repetitive queries, leading to delayed response times and **abandoned carts.**

AI Solution:

> "Create an AI-powered chatbot script that answers FAQs, recommends products based on skin type, and upsells bundles."

Results:

- **40% reduction** in support tickets.
- **25% increase** in cart conversion rate.
- AI-driven personalized recommendations **boosted average order value by 18%.**

🔥 **Key Takeaway:** AI-powered customer support **isn't just about answering questions—it's a conversion machine.**

Case Study 3: Using AI for Competitive Intelligence

Company: Enterprise SaaS startup

Problem: The sales team needed to **track competitors in real-time** but lacked the bandwidth to manually monitor industry shifts.

AI Solution:

> "Create a competitive analysis report summarizing recent moves by our top 5 competitors. Include product launches, funding rounds, and strategic partnerships."

Results:

- AI-generated reports gave the sales team **real-time insights.**
- Allowed faster **counter-messaging against competitors.**
- Increased sales team's **win rate by 15%.**

🔥 **Key Takeaway:** AI **turns data into strategy—faster than any human could.**

7.3 Key Lessons from Real-World Applications

Across industries, DeepSeek is **not just a tool—it's a force multiplier.** Here's what we've learned from these applications:

1️⃣ **AI saves time, but only if prompted correctly.**

- Weak prompts = weak results.
- Structured prompts = **AI that actually delivers.**

2️⃣ **AI amplifies human expertise—it doesn't replace it.**

- Lawyers still review contracts, but AI does the **heavy lifting.**
- Marketers still write copy, but AI **accelerates ideation.**
- CEOs still make decisions, but AI **provides better data.**

3️⃣ **Businesses that use AI strategically gain a massive competitive advantage.**

- The firms leveraging AI today **are the market leaders of tomorrow.**
- AI isn't a futuristic tool—it's a **right-now** tool.

Final Thoughts: You're Now a High-Level AI Practitioner

At this point, you're not just playing with AI—you're **deploying it in real-world scenarios.**

What separates AI **amateurs** from **pros?**

- Amateurs run random prompts and hope for good results.
- **Pros use structured techniques, frameworks, and iteration.**

🚀 **Next Up: Optimizing for DeepSeek's Unique Features** The next chapter will show you **how to push DeepSeek even further**, maximizing its reasoning capabilities, efficiency, and output precision.

Chapter 8: Optimizing for DeepSeek's Unique Features

At this stage, you're beyond basic prompting—you're operating at a level where **every prompt is an investment.** You're not just getting *good* AI responses; you're **squeezing every last drop of value out of DeepSeek's capabilities.**

This chapter is all about **fine-tuning** your approach to maximize DeepSeek's unique features—**reasoning power, efficiency, structured output control, and cost-free optimization.**

8.1 Maximizing R1's Reasoning Power

DeepSeek's **R1 model is a reasoning powerhouse.** Unlike some LLMs that flounder on multi-step logic, **DeepSeek thrives when you challenge it with complex, structured problems.** But only **if you prompt it correctly.**

Step 1: Force Logical Structuring with Chain-of-Thought

🚫 **Basic Prompt:**

> "What are the benefits of intermittent fasting?"

🤖 *AI gives a generic response—probably listing 3-4 benefits without depth.*

⬛ **Better Prompt (CoT Applied):**

> "Explain the benefits of intermittent fasting in a structured manner. First, define intermittent fasting. Then, list and explain five key physiological benefits, citing scientific reasoning behind each."

🔥 **Why this works:**

- You're **forcing logical organization.**
- The AI is encouraged to think step-by-step instead of dumping facts.
- The output is **instantly more usable and insightful.**

Step 2: Deep Dives with Recursive Inquiry

🚫 **Shallow Prompt:**

> "Explain blockchain."

🤖 *AI spits out a surface-level summary.*

⬛ **Recursive Prompting Fix:**

> "Explain blockchain as if I'm a beginner.
> Now, deepen the explanation by adding an
> example of how Bitcoin uses blockchain.
> Next, analyze its impact on financial
> decentralization."

🔥 **Why this works:**

- Each step **builds on the previous one.**
- The AI is forced to **move from basic to advanced concepts.**
- Instead of stopping at a simple answer, it **keeps expanding depth.**

Pro Tip: If you're getting shallow answers, **manually push the AI deeper** with follow-up recursive prompts like:

- *"Expand on the last point with a real-world example."*
- *"Now explain why this matters in practical applications."*
- *"What are the counterarguments to this perspective?"*

8.2 Cost-Free Efficiency: Getting More from Free-Tier AI

DeepSeek is **free**—but that doesn't mean you should be wasteful with your queries. Efficiency is key. The best AI users optimize **both cost and output quality.**

How to Get the Most Out of Free AI Access

1 Batch Your Queries

- Instead of running 10 small prompts, **consolidate them into structured multi-part prompts**.
- 🚀 **Example:** Instead of asking 5 different questions about marketing strategies, use:

  "Provide five high-impact marketing strategies for SaaS companies, explaining each in detail."

2 Use Output Compression

- If you're generating long responses, **force summaries upfront.**
- 🚀 **Example:**

  "Summarize this response in three bullet points after your full explanation."

- This gives you a **quick reference** instead of re-reading the full response.

③ Predefine Output Structure

- Instead of getting an unstructured response and fixing it later, **force DeepSeek to format it for you.**
- 🚀 **Example:**

  "List five key business trends in 2025. For each, include: (1) a brief explanation, (2) a real-world example, and (3) its expected market impact."

- Now, the AI doesn't just **dump data—it organizes it from the start.**

🔥 Why this matters:

- You **reduce unnecessary back-and-forth.**
- You **get clean, structured answers immediately.**
- You **maximize the free-tier without wasting queries.**

8.3 Customizing Output Formats

Most AI users **manually reformat** AI responses. That's a waste of time. **Smart AI users make the AI do the formatting for them.**

Output as JSON (For Developers & Automation)

⊘ Bad Prompt:

"List the top AI companies."

AI gives a simple text list.

Optimized Prompt:

"List the top AI companies and format the response in JSON. Include: name, headquarters, primary AI focus, and notable product."

Now you get structured JSON output ready for automation.

Output as Markdown (For Content Creators)

⊘ Messy Prompt:

"Summarize AI trends in 2025."

Markdown-Optimized Prompt:

> "Summarize AI trends in 2025. Format the response in Markdown with H2 headers, bullet points, and bold key terms."

👍 *Now your content is **instantly ready for publishing.***

Output in Tables (For Business & Analysis)

🚫 Unstructured Output:

> "Compare Tesla, Google, and OpenAI."

⬛ Better Prompt:

> "Compare Tesla, Google, and OpenAI in a markdown table with columns: 'Company', 'Focus Area', 'AI Innovations', and 'Market Influence'."

👍 *Now you get a clear, structured table instead of a jumbled paragraph.*

🔥 Key Takeaway:

- **Never reformat AI output manually**—tell the AI what format you need **before it generates text.**

Final Thoughts: Becoming a DeepSeek Power User

DeepSeek is **already one of the most powerful free-tier AIs available.** But **only if you use it right.**

🚀 **Key Takeaways from Chapter 8:**
[1]**Use Chain-of-Thought and Recursive Prompting** to force logical, structured responses.
[2]**Batch and Compress Queries** to maximize **free-tier efficiency.**
[3]**Predefine Output Structure** (JSON, Markdown, Tables) to **save hours of manual formatting.**

Most people **waste time fighting AI.** You now know how to make AI **work for you.**

Next Up: Ethical Considerations

With great power comes great responsibility. The next chapter dives into **AI ethics, bias mitigation, and how to ensure AI-generated content remains fair, balanced, and ethical.**

Because using AI effectively **isn't just about power—it's about responsibility.**

Chapter 9: Ethical Considerations in AI Usage

At this point, you have the skills to **wield AI like a precision instrument**—but with great power comes great responsibility. Just because you *can* make AI do something doesn't always mean you *should*.

This chapter dives into **AI ethics, bias mitigation, and ensuring fairness in AI-generated content.** Mastering AI isn't just about maximizing performance; it's about using it in ways that are **ethical, responsible, and aligned with human values.**

9.1 Understanding AI Bias: Why It Happens

AI models don't *think*—they pattern-match based on their training data. This means that if the data is biased, **the AI will be biased too.**

How Bias Creeps Into AI

1. **Training Data Bias** – AI models learn from vast datasets, which often include historical biases present in society.
2. **Reinforcement Bias** – If users reward biased outputs, models may continue generating them.
3. **Omission Bias** – Sometimes, AI avoids discussing controversial topics, leading to gaps in information.
4. **Algorithmic Bias** – AI's probability-based reasoning can reinforce existing societal inequalities.

🚀 **Example:**

- If AI is trained mostly on Western literature, it may underrepresent perspectives from other cultures.
- If AI is trained on job application data where certain groups were historically underrepresented, it may suggest biased hiring recommendations.

Understanding these biases is **the first step to counteracting them.**

9.2 How to Mitigate AI Bias in Your Prompts

You can't fully eliminate AI bias, but you **can control it** with smart prompting techniques.

Strategy 1: Explicitly Ask for Balanced Perspectives

⊘ Biased Prompt:

"Why is remote work bad for productivity?"

◼ Bias-Mitigating Prompt:

"Discuss the pros and cons of remote work on productivity, citing evidence from different industries."

🔥 Why this works:

- It forces the AI to **present multiple perspectives.**
- It reduces the chance of the model reinforcing **one-sided arguments.**

Strategy 2: Include Diverse Examples

⊘ Narrow Prompt:

"Give me leadership strategies from Fortune 500 CEOs."

◼ Inclusive Prompt:

"Provide leadership strategies from successful leaders in both Fortune 500 companies and small businesses globally."

🔥 **Why this works:**

- AI broadens its response instead of defaulting to the most prominent (often Western, male-dominated) examples.

Strategy 3: Use AI to Check Itself

AI can **audit its own biases** if you ask the right way.

⬛ **Meta-Prompt:**

"Analyze this response for potential bias. Are there perspectives that might be missing?"

🔥 **Why this works:**

- AI highlights its own gaps, helping you **catch blind spots.**

9.3 Transparency & Accountability in AI Usage

Transparency is key when using AI-generated content, especially in business, journalism, and research.

When Should You Disclose AI Usage?

🚀 **Best Practices:**

- If AI-generated content influences **public decision-making** (e.g., journalism, legal documents, policy reports), transparency is **mandatory.**
- In creative work (e.g., blog posts, ad copy), disclose AI assistance **if it significantly contributed to the final product.**
- In internal tasks (e.g., brainstorming, summarization), disclosure is **optional but recommended** for clarity.

🚫 **Bad Practice:** Using AI-generated content verbatim without review or disclosure.

⬛ **Good Practice:**

> "This article was drafted with AI assistance and fact-checked by a human editor."

9.4 Ethical Considerations in AI-Generated Decision-Making

AI is being used to make decisions in **hiring, law enforcement, lending, and healthcare.** But what happens when those decisions are flawed?

Example: AI in Hiring

⃠ Unethical Scenario:

- AI scans resumes and **systematically filters out** applicants from certain backgrounds due to historical biases in hiring data.

◼ Ethical Fix:

- AI should be used to **augment** hiring decisions, not fully automate them.
- Human oversight is required to **review AI-generated recommendations.**

Example: AI in Criminal Justice

⃠ Unethical Scenario:

- Predictive policing AI disproportionately flags certain neighborhoods, reinforcing systemic inequalities.

◼ Ethical Fix:

- AI should be trained on **diverse, fair datasets** and monitored for disparities.

9.5 AI and Data Privacy: What You Need to Know

AI **processes massive amounts of data**—but how it handles privacy is crucial.

Best Practices for AI Data Ethics

■ **Ensure Consent** – If AI is analyzing personal data, ensure **explicit user consent.**

■ **Minimize Data Retention** – Only store data as long as necessary.

■ **Avoid Personally Identifiable Information (PII)** – Don't prompt AI to generate or analyze sensitive data without safeguards.

🚀 **Example:**

- **Bad Practice:** "Analyze this customer's chat history to predict their future purchases."
- **Good Practice:** "Analyze anonymized customer trends to predict future product demand."

9.6 Ethical AI Usage in Content Creation

AI can generate everything from blog posts to deepfake videos—but ethical AI usage requires boundaries.

What's Ethical?

■ Using AI to assist in idea generation, drafting, and research. ■ Disclosing when AI-generated content plays a major role. ■ Fact-checking AI-generated claims.

What's Unethical?

⃠ Passing off AI-generated work as 100% human-created without review. ⃠ Using AI to spread misinformation. ⃠ Manipulating AI to create deceptive or harmful content.

🔥 **Golden Rule:** AI should **enhance creativity and efficiency**, not replace ethical judgment.

Final Thoughts: AI as a Responsible Tool

AI is an **unstoppable force**—but its impact depends on how we use it.

🚀 **Key Takeaways from Chapter 9:**
1️⃣ **Bias exists in AI, but you can counteract it** through thoughtful prompting.
2️⃣ **Transparency matters—disclose AI usage when appropriate.**
3️⃣ **AI should assist, not replace, human judgment in decision-making.**
4️⃣ **Data privacy and ethical content creation are non-negotiable.**

Using AI responsibly isn't just about compliance—it's about **ensuring the technology serves humanity, not the other way around.**

Next Up: Tools & Resources for AI Mastery

You now understand both **the power and the responsibility** of AI. The next chapter will equip you with **the best tools, prompt libraries, and communities** to stay at the cutting edge of AI mastery.

Let's gear up for **the final phase of your AI journey.**

Chapter 10: Tools & Resources for AI Mastery

By now, you understand **how to craft powerful prompts, optimize AI outputs, and apply DeepSeek in real-world scenarios.** But mastery isn't just about knowing what to do—it's about having the right tools to execute at the highest level.

This chapter is your **toolkit for AI mastery.** We'll cover the best resources, prompt libraries, and automation tools to help you **work smarter, scale faster, and stay ahead of the AI curve.**

10.1 Prompt Libraries: Pre-Built Powerhouses

A **great prompt is a shortcut to a great output.** Instead of crafting prompts from scratch every time, leverage **pre-built libraries** to get instant results.

Best Prompt Libraries

■ **DeepSeek Prompt Hub** – A curated collection of optimized prompts specifically designed for DeepSeek's capabilities. ■ **Awesome ChatGPT Prompts** – A GitHub repository with thousands of categorized prompts. ■ **PromptBase** – A marketplace for high-quality, pre-tested prompts for different AI models. ■ **FlowGPT** – A dynamic prompt-sharing platform where users upload and rate effective AI prompts.

🚀 **Pro Tip: Don't just copy-paste prompts.** Use them as **templates** and refine them based on **your specific needs.**

10.2 AI Tools for Enhanced Productivity

If you're serious about AI, you need **more than just a chatbot.** These tools **supercharge AI workflows** by integrating with DeepSeek and other LLMs.

AI-Powered Writing Assistants

■ **Notion AI** – Turns Notion into an AI-driven knowledge base and writing assistant. ■ **Grammarly + AI** – Improves grammar, tone, and clarity with AI-powered suggestions. ■ **Jasper AI** – A dedicated content-generation AI tailored for marketing and copywriting.

AI Code Assistants

■ **GitHub Copilot** – AI-powered coding companion for developers. ■ **DeepSeek R1** – Exceptional for debugging, refactoring, and optimizing code. ■ **Codeium** – Free alternative to Copilot, offering strong AI-assisted coding features.

AI Research & Summarization Tools

■ **Elicit** – Uses AI to find, summarize, and analyze research papers. ■ **Perplexity AI** – Advanced AI search engine that provides deeper insights than Google. ■ **ChatPDF** – AI-driven tool for summarizing and querying PDFs instantly.

🚀 **Pro Tip:** Stack these tools together to **automate complex workflows**—like using DeepSeek for idea generation and Notion AI for final edits.

10.3 Automation & No-Code AI Tools

Why do things manually when **AI can automate them?** These **no-code automation tools** let you integrate AI into **business processes, workflows, and creative projects—without writing a single line of code.**

Best No-Code AI Platforms

■ **Zapier + AI Actions** – Automate repetitive tasks using AI-driven workflows. ■ **Make.com** – Advanced no-code automation that connects AI with business applications. ■ **OpenAI API Playground** – Experiment with AI capabilities in a sandbox environment. ■ **Replit AI** – An AI-powered cloud development environment for coding automation.

🚀 **Use Case Example:**

- Automate customer support: **Use Zapier to integrate DeepSeek with Slack & Gmail for AI-generated email responses.**
- Automate content creation: **Generate blog outlines with DeepSeek, pass them to Notion AI, and auto-publish with Zapier.**

The future isn't just AI—it's AI-powered automation.

10.4 AI Communities & Knowledge Hubs

AI is evolving **faster than any technology in history.** If you want to stay ahead, you need to be plugged into **the right communities and knowledge sources.**

Best AI Communities

■ **DeepSeek Discord** – Connect with other power users and developers optimizing DeepSeek. ■ **r/LocalLLaMA & r/ArtificialIntelligence (Reddit)** – Forums for discussing AI advancements and sharing prompting strategies. ■ **EleutherAI** – A leading open-source AI research community pushing the boundaries of AI development. ■ **Hugging Face** – The best place for open-source AI models, datasets, and discussions.

Must-Read AI Newsletters

■ **Import AI (Jack Clark)** – Deep insights into AI advancements and ethical discussions. ■ **The AI Alignment Newsletter** – Focuses on AI safety, ethics, and the future of AGI. ■ **Ben's Bites** – A daily AI digest that summarizes the latest AI news in bite-sized pieces.

🚀 **Pro Tip:** Join AI communities **not just to learn—but to contribute.** The best way to master AI is by engaging with experts and sharing insights.

10.5 Staying Ahead: How to Future-Proof Your AI Skills

AI is **not slowing down.** If anything, it's evolving at **exponential speed.** The question isn't whether AI will change the world—the question is **whether you'll keep up.**

How to Stay on the Cutting Edge

1 **Experiment with New Models** – Always test the latest LLMs, including DeepSeek updates and open-source models like Mistral & Llama.

2 **Contribute to AI Research** – Even if you're not a researcher, contributing insights, feedback, or datasets improves AI for everyone.

3 **Build & Automate** – Whether you're a coder or not, learn to integrate AI into real-world applications (Zapier, API automation, etc.).

4 **Keep Learning** – The AI landscape shifts **weekly.** Stay adaptable by reading, engaging in discussions, and testing new workflows.

🚀 **Final Thought:**

> The people who win in the AI revolution aren't the ones who *consume AI*—they're the ones who *create with AI.*

Final Thoughts: You Are Now an AI Power User

You've completed **an entire journey through AI mastery.** From the fundamentals of prompt engineering to **real-world applications, ethical considerations, and advanced automation techniques**—you now possess a skill set that **most people will never develop.**

💡 What Separates AI Amateurs from AI Pros?

- **Amateurs use AI passively.**
- **Pros integrate AI strategically into their workflows.**
- **Masters automate, optimize, and scale AI-driven solutions.**

🚀 Where Do You Go From Here?

1. **Start Implementing** – Pick at least **three AI tools** from this chapter and integrate them into your workflow.
2. **Join AI Communities** – Engage in discussions, share insights, and learn from other power users.
3. **Experiment Relentlessly** – The more you test and refine your prompts, the better your AI outputs will be.

The AI revolution is happening **now**—and you are **at the forefront of it.**

Congratulations. You are no longer just an AI user. You are an **AI architect, an automation strategist, and a power player in the future of technology.**

Welcome to the new era. Let's build the future.

Chapter 11: Conclusion & Next Steps

You've made it to the end of this guide, but the real journey is just beginning.

Mastering AI and DeepSeek isn't about memorizing techniques—it's about continuously **experimenting, adapting, and evolving.** The landscape of AI changes **daily**, and the people who thrive in this space are the ones who stay **curious, proactive, and always learning.**

This chapter will summarize the key takeaways from this guide, outline your **next steps**, and set you up for long-term AI success.

11.1 The Core Lessons You Should Take Away

Over the last ten chapters, you've learned **how to turn DeepSeek into an unstoppable force multiplier.** Here are the core takeaways you should always keep in mind:

🚀 The Four Pillars of AI Mastery

[1] **Precision Prompting Wins** – The quality of your AI output **is only as good as your input.**

- Be clear, structured, and intentional with every prompt.
- Use frameworks like RACE, TAG, and STEP to refine your results.
- Iterate—great AI outputs rarely come on the first try.

[2] **DeepSeek Is a Reasoning Powerhouse** – Unlike other models, DeepSeek excels in **structured logic, problem-solving, and deep analysis.**

- Use **Chain-of-Thought (CoT) prompting** for multi-step reasoning.
- Apply **recursive prompting** to dive deeper into complex topics.
- Optimize its strengths—DeepSeek is not just a chatbot; it's a strategic tool.

[3] **AI Is a Partner, Not a Replacement** – The best AI users **augment their work with AI, not replace their thinking.**

- AI **automates repetitive tasks**, but critical thinking is still your superpower.
- Treat AI as an **intelligent assistant**—it can enhance, but you control the final output.
- The best AI practitioners use **human-AI collaboration** to get exponential results.

4 **Ethics and Responsibility Matter** – AI is a tool of **immense power**, and with that comes responsibility.

- **Bias is real**—always ask AI to provide multiple perspectives.
- **Transparency matters**—if AI generates significant content, disclose it.
- **Privacy and data ethics**—don't use AI in ways that compromise personal data or ethics.

11.2 The Road Ahead: What's Next?

You're not just an AI user anymore—you're an **AI strategist, a power user, and a creator.** The question is: **what's next?**

📌 Step 1: Integrate AI Into Your Daily Workflows

"AI is only useful if it's applied."

Take the knowledge from this book and **start applying it immediately.** Whether you're in marketing, business, programming, research, or creative work, **AI can give you leverage.**

• **For Business & Strategy:** Automate reports, run competitor analysis, and optimize decision-making. ✦ **For Creators & Writers:** Use AI to generate ideas, streamline content creation, and improve storytelling. ✦ **For Developers:** Let DeepSeek assist in debugging, refactoring, and structuring better code. ✦ **For Researchers:** Summarize papers, extract key trends, and deepen analytical thinking.

The fastest way to **get better at AI is to use it in real-world scenarios.**

📌 Step 2: Join the AI Community & Stay Updated

> "AI evolves at an insane speed. The only way to stay ahead is to stay connected."

• **Join AI Communities:** Engage in AI discussions, share prompting strategies, and collaborate.

- DeepSeek Discord (If it's still around)
- Hugging Face AI Forum
- r/ArtificialIntelligence on Reddit

• **Follow AI Thought Leaders:** Stay ahead by learning from the best.

- OpenAI Research Blog
- DeepSeek AI Updates

- AI research papers on arXiv

◆ **Experiment With New AI Models:** DeepSeek is powerful, but so are **other AI advancements.** Stay updated with:

- GPT models
- Open-source LLMs (Mistral, Llama, Falcon)
- AI-powered automation tools

AI mastery is a **lifelong skill.** Keep testing, iterating, and improving.

📌 Step 3: Build AI-Driven Projects & Automations

> "AI mastery isn't about using AI—it's about building with AI."

To truly leverage AI, move beyond just **prompting** and start **building.**

🚀 Project Ideas to Get Started:

- Automate repetitive tasks in your job using **Zapier + DeepSeek.**
- Build an AI-driven research assistant to summarize industry news.
- Create a **personal AI chatbot** tailored to your workflow.

- Develop a **custom AI prompt library** to improve team efficiency.
- Train AI on your own datasets to create **domain-specific knowledge assistants.**

The real power of AI isn't in asking better questions—it's in designing systems that produce better answers.

11.3 Final Words: The Future Is AI-Powered, and You're Ready

If there's one thing you should take away from this book, it's this:

> **AI isn't replacing you. But someone using AI better than you might.**

🚀 The difference between people who thrive in the AI revolution and those who get left behind isn't **access to AI—it's skill in using it.**

You now have the knowledge, the techniques, and the strategies to **outperform 99% of AI users.** But knowledge alone won't make you great—**execution will.**

The world is changing fast, and AI is leading the charge. But instead of fearing disruption, **you are now one of the disruptors.**

This is your moment.

Go build. Go create. Go innovate.

Welcome to the future.

Bonus Content

We'll be covering quick references here, as well as Prompt Engineering terms, FAQ's, and a few "fill in the blank" prompts.

Appendix A: Cheat Sheet – Quick Reference for AI Prompting

This cheat sheet is your **instant-access guide** to mastering AI prompting. Whether you need to generate structured responses, debug bad outputs, or refine your queries for maximum precision, **this is your go-to resource.**

🔥 The Golden Rules of Prompting

■ **Be Specific** – The more precise your prompt, the better the output.
■ **Provide Context** – Give AI the necessary background to generate useful responses.

■ Use Examples – Show AI what you want by including sample outputs.
■ Define Output Format – Specify JSON, bullet points, markdown, etc., for structured responses.
■ Iterate & Refine – Don't settle for the first answer—improve it with follow-ups.
■ Guide AI with Roles – Assign AI a role to influence response style (e.g., *"Act as a business analyst…"*).

🔍 Frameworks for Effective Prompts

⬤ RACE Framework (Role, Action, Context, Examples)

Use for structured, logical AI responses.

■ Example:

"You are a cybersecurity expert. Write a risk assessment report on cloud security vulnerabilities. Include real-world case studies and best practices."

🏆 TAG Method (Task, Audience, Goal)

Use for clear, audience-targeted responses.

⬛ **Example:**

"Summarize the latest AI research for non-technical executives. Focus on business impact and future trends."

⚡ STEP Approach (Specify, Test, Evaluate, Polish)

Use for iterative refinement of AI responses.

⬛ **Example:**

S: "Draft an email for a product launch."
T: "Improve clarity and engagement."
E: "Check tone and persuasiveness."
P: "Polish for conciseness and impact."

🛠️ Quick Fixes for Bad AI Responses

🚫 **Too Generic?** → Add depth: *"Explain in detail with industry-specific examples."*
🚫 **Too Long?** → Force brevity: *"Summarize in 3 key points."*
🚫 **Too Complex?** → Simplify: *"Explain as if talking to a 12-year-old."*
🚫 **Incorrect Info?** → Verify: *"Cite sources and explain reasoning."*
🚫 **Lacks Creativity?** → Enhance style: *"Make it more engaging and humorous."*

📂 Output Formatting Shortcuts

1️⃣ **Bullet Points:** *"Summarize in bullet points."*
▪️ **Tables:** *"Create a markdown table comparing Tesla, Google, and OpenAI."*
▪️ **JSON:** *"Format response in JSON with 'title', 'author', and 'summary' fields."*
🎤 **Quotes:** *"Use direct quotes from industry leaders."*
▪️ **Charts & Data:** *"List five AI trends and their adoption rates in a markdown table."*

🚀 Advanced Techniques

■ Chain-of-Thought (CoT) Prompting

Use for logical step-by-step reasoning.

■ Example:

"Explain the impact of inflation step by step, from causes to economic consequences."

■ Recursive Prompting

Use when AI needs to refine its own output.

■ Example:

"Now refine your answer for conciseness and clarity."

🐑 Multi-Agent Prompting

Use for debates, comparisons, and simulated expert discussions.

■ Example:

"Simulate a debate between a tech CEO supporting remote work and an economist arguing against it."

💡 Quick Prompts for Common Use Cases

📌 **Marketing:** *"Write a persuasive LinkedIn post about the future of AI in business."*
📌 **Business Analysis:** *"Conduct a SWOT analysis for Tesla's expansion into robotics."*
📌 **Research Summaries:** *"Summarize this 20-page report in 5 bullet points."*
📌 **Coding Help:** *"Explain this Python error message and suggest a fix."*
📌 **Creative Writing:** *"Write a sci-fi short story about AI and human coexistence."*
📌 **Decision-Making:** *"List the pros and cons of outsourcing software development."*

🚩 Final Thoughts

Mastering AI prompting is about control. The best prompters don't just accept **whatever AI gives them**—they **shape it, refine it, and optimize it.**

Appendix B: Glossary – Key AI & Prompt Engineering Terms

This glossary serves as a **quick-reference guide** to key terms and concepts used throughout this book. If you ever need a refresher on AI terminology or prompting strategies, **this is the section to consult.**

🔥 Core AI Concepts

🤖 Artificial Intelligence (AI)

The simulation of human intelligence in machines, enabling them to **learn, reason, and make decisions**.

🧠 Large Language Model (LLM)

A type of AI trained on massive text datasets to generate **coherent, human-like text responses**.

 Machine Learning (ML)

A subset of AI that enables computers to **learn from data** and improve their performance over time **without explicit programming**.

⚙ Deep Learning

A specialized form of machine learning that uses **neural networks with multiple layers** to process complex patterns in data.

🔍 Natural Language Processing (NLP)

A field of AI focused on enabling machines to **understand, interpret, and generate human language**.

⚡ AI Prompting & Response Techniques

● Prompt Engineering

The strategic design of inputs to optimize **LLM responses for accuracy, clarity, and relevance**.

■ Chain-of-Thought (CoT) Prompting

A prompting technique that instructs AI to break down its reasoning into **step-by-step explanations**.

■ Example: *"Explain how inflation works step by step."*

■ Recursive Prompting

A method where you **refine AI responses** by asking it to build upon or improve its previous answers.

■ Example: *"Now simplify your explanation further for a 10-year-old."*

🐾 Role-Based Prompting

Assigning AI a **specific role or persona** to influence response tone and style.

■ Example: *"You are a financial analyst. Summarize this stock market trend."*

🔥 Multi-Agent Prompting

A technique where AI generates **multiple perspectives** in a simulated conversation.

■ Example: *"Debate the pros and cons of universal basic income from an economist and a policy maker's viewpoint."*

■ Few-Shot Prompting

Providing **a few examples** to guide AI's response quality and format.

■ **Example:** *"Generate an engaging Instagram caption. Examples: 'Rise & grind!* ☀ *#MorningMotivation', 'Coffee first, strategy second.* ☕ *#Hustle'"*

◤ AI Output Formatting & Optimization

◤ Structured Formatting

Controlling AI output structure using **specific instructions.**

■ **Example:** *"List five key startup funding strategies in bullet points."*

■ Tabular Output

Forcing AI to organize responses in **table format for better readability.**

■ **Example:** *"Create a markdown table comparing Tesla, Google, and OpenAI in terms of market impact."*

■ JSON Formatting

Using AI to generate structured **machine-readable** outputs in JSON.

■ Example: *"List the top AI research papers in JSON format with 'title', 'author', and 'summary' fields."*

📌 Meta-Prompting

Using AI to **improve its own prompts** by asking for refinements.

■ Example: *"Rewrite this prompt to make it clearer and more specific: 'Explain deep learning.'"*

🏗 AI Ethics & Safety Terms

⚖️ Bias Mitigation

Techniques used to **reduce AI-generated biases** by adjusting prompts or training datasets.

🔎 Transparency in AI

Ensuring that AI users **disclose** when content is AI-generated and clarify potential limitations.

📽 AI Data Privacy

Ethical considerations around **how AI models handle, store, and use data**.

▌ Algorithmic Fairness

Developing AI models that **do not favor or discriminate unfairly** against any group.

⬤ AI Hallucination

When AI generates **false, misleading, or entirely fabricated** information that sounds convincing.

▌ **Example:** *If AI claims "Elon Musk founded OpenAI," that's a hallucination—he was an early funder, not the founder.*

🚀 Quick AI Use Cases & Terminology

▊ Business & Strategy AI Applications

- **Market Analysis AI** – Uses AI to analyze industry trends and consumer behavior.
- **AI-Powered Competitive Intelligence** – Automates tracking of competitor movements.
- **Business Forecasting AI** – Predicts revenue, market shifts, and industry risks.

📣 Marketing & Content AI Applications

- **AI-Powered Copywriting** – Generates persuasive sales and marketing copy.
- **SEO Content Optimization** – Enhances blog articles for search engines.
- **Social Media AI** – Automates content scheduling and engagement.

🏗 AI for Developers

- **Code Autocompletion AI** – Tools like GitHub Copilot suggest code snippets.
- **AI Debugging Assistant** – AI identifies and fixes code errors.
- **Low-Code/No-Code AI** – Enables app development without advanced coding skills.

🔬 AI for Research & Analysis

- **AI Summarization Tools** – Condense lengthy research papers into digestible insights.
- **Data-Driven Insights AI** – Extracts patterns from large datasets.
- **AI-Powered Citation Analysis** – Finds related academic papers based on key topics.

🚩 Final Thoughts: AI Literacy = AI Power

This glossary **isn't just a list of terms—it's your survival guide** in the AI revolution. The more fluent you are in these concepts, the more **effective, efficient, and powerful your AI-driven work will be.**

AI isn't just a tool; **it's a new language.** Now, you speak it fluently.

Appendix C: FAQ – Common Questions About AI & Prompt Engineering

This section answers the **most frequently asked questions** about AI, DeepSeek, and advanced prompt engineering. Whether you're troubleshooting issues, refining your prompting strategies, or looking for AI best practices, **this is your quick-reference guide.**

General AI Questions

What is the difference between AI, Machine Learning, and Deep Learning?

- **AI (Artificial Intelligence):** The broad field of making machines perform tasks that typically require human intelligence.
- **Machine Learning (ML):** A subset of AI where machines learn patterns from data without being explicitly programmed.

- **Deep Learning:** A specialized type of ML that uses **neural networks with multiple layers** to process complex patterns.

⬤ How does DeepSeek compare to GPT-4o or Claude?

DeepSeek R1 is a **reasoning-optimized LLM** that excels in **structured problem-solving, logical analysis, and efficiency.** Compared to:

- **GPT-4o:** More generalized, better at natural conversation but slightly weaker in structured logic.
- **Claude:** Strong memory and context retention, but DeepSeek outperforms it in step-by-step reasoning.

◼ Can DeepSeek replace human decision-making?

No. AI should be used as an **assistant, not a replacement.** It's powerful for analysis, brainstorming, and automation but still lacks human intuition, judgment, and ethical considerations.

⚡ Prompt Engineering FAQs

⬤ Why does my AI output seem too generic?

🚀 **Fix:** Your prompt is likely **too broad** or **under-specified.** ⬛ **Solution:** Add **constraints, examples, or role-based instructions** to refine results.

Example: Instead of *"Explain SEO"*, try:

> "Explain SEO for small business owners, focusing on local search ranking factors. Use real-world case studies."

⬛ How can I get AI to follow a step-by-step reasoning process?

Use **Chain-of-Thought (CoT) prompting.**

⬛ Example:

> "Explain how inflation works. Start with the definition, then list three causes, followed by its impact on consumers."

This forces AI to **think in logical steps** instead of providing shallow responses.

🏗 How do I get AI to write in a specific style?

Use **Role-Based Prompting.**

■ Example:

> "You are a financial journalist writing for Bloomberg. Explain the latest stock market trends in an engaging yet professional tone."

🚀 Troubleshooting AI Issues

▲ Why does AI sometimes ignore my instructions?

🚀 **Fix:** AI models prioritize high-probability responses based on training data. To fix this:

1. **Reinforce instructions.** Repeat key details at the end of your prompt.
2. **Use explicit constraints.** Tell AI what *not* to do.
3. **Iterate.** If the first response isn't right, refine and re-run.

■ Example Fix:

> "List five startup funding strategies. Keep each explanation under 50 words. Do NOT include crowdfunding."

🪲 Why does AI hallucinate (make up facts)?

All LLMs **predict text based on probability, not fact-checking.** This means AI might confidently generate false information.

⬛ Fix:

- **Ask for sources**: *"Cite reputable sources for your answer."*
- **Use verification prompts**: *"Double-check this response for accuracy and correct any errors."*
- **Cross-reference outputs**: Run the same query across different AI models.

⬤ How do I prevent biased or unethical AI responses?

🚀 **Fix:** AI learns from biased datasets, but you can counteract this by:

1. **Asking for diverse perspectives**: *"Provide arguments for and against remote work."*
2. **Challenging assumptions**: *"Does this answer contain any biases? If so, correct them."*
3. **Fact-checking manually** before relying on AI-generated insights.

⚑ AI Use Cases & Best Practices

■ How can businesses integrate AI efficiently?

- Automate repetitive tasks (email responses, scheduling, data entry).
- Enhance research (summarization, industry analysis, competitive intelligence).
- Improve customer service (AI chatbots, support ticket classification).
- Generate marketing content (ad copy, blog posts, SEO optimization).

■ What are the best AI tools to pair with DeepSeek?

■ **For writing & content:** Notion AI, Grammarly, Jasper AI ■ **For coding & development:** GitHub Copilot, DeepSeek R1, Codeium ■ **For research & automation:** Perplexity AI, Elicit, Zapier + AI Actions

🔎 How do I optimize AI responses for structured output?

Use **predefined formatting instructions.**

■ Example:

"Summarize the five biggest AI trends of 2025 in a markdown table with three columns: Trend, Impact, and Industry Application."

This forces AI to **deliver structured, usable results.**

🏴 Final Thoughts: AI as an Everyday Tool

Mastering AI isn't just about knowing **how** to prompt—it's about knowing **how to troubleshoot, refine, and optimize AI workflows.**

🚀 Key Takeaways:

1. **Refine your prompts** when AI responses are weak.
2. **Use structured outputs** to get precise results.
3. **Verify facts & mitigate bias** to ensure accuracy.
4. **Integrate AI into daily workflows** for maximum leverage.

AI is the **ultimate productivity tool**—but only if you know **how to use it effectively.**

Now that you have this FAQ as your troubleshooting guide, you're equipped to **handle any AI challenge that comes your way.**

Appendix D: Prompt Templates – Fill-in-the-Blank AI Commands

This section provides **ready-to-use, high-performance prompt templates** for different use cases. Whether you're generating content, analyzing data, or refining AI responses, these templates give you **instant leverage.**

▰ Writing & Content Creation Prompts

📣 Social Media Marketing

▰ Template:

> "Write a high-engagement [platform] post about [topic]. Use a tone that is [casual/professional/humorous]. Include a call to action encouraging [engagement type]."

Example:

"Write a high-engagement LinkedIn post about the future of AI in business. Use a professional tone. Include a call to action encouraging discussion."

🏆 SEO-Optimized Blog Posts

■ Template:

"Write an SEO-friendly blog post about [topic]. Target the keyword [keyword]. The post should be [word count] long and include sections on [main points]."

Example:

"Write an SEO-friendly blog post about 'The Benefits of Remote Work.' Target the keyword 'remote work productivity.' The post should be 1,500 words long and include sections on flexibility, employee happiness, and cost savings."

🛍 Product Descriptions

■ Template:

"Write a compelling product description for [product]. Highlight its key benefits, features, and ideal use cases. Keep it under [word count] words."

Example:

"Write a compelling product description for a noise-canceling wireless headphone. Highlight its key benefits, features, and ideal use cases. Keep it under 100 words."

◼ Business & Analytical Prompts

◼ Market Research Reports

◼ Template:

"Generate a market analysis report for [industry]. Include insights on current trends, major competitors, and future predictions."

Example:

"Generate a market analysis report for the electric vehicle industry. Include insights on

current trends, major competitors, and
future predictions."

🔍 Competitor Analysis

⬛ Template:

"Compare [Company A] with [Company B].
Create a table listing differences in [criteria:
pricing, product features, target audience,
etc.]."

Example:

"Compare Tesla with Rivian. Create a table
listing differences in pricing, product
features, and market positioning."

⚫ SWOT Analysis

⬛ Template:

"Conduct a SWOT analysis for
[company/product/strategy]. Focus on
strengths, weaknesses, opportunities, and
threats."

Example:

"Conduct a SWOT analysis for Apple's expansion into AR/VR technology."

■ AI Optimization & Debugging Prompts

⚒ Refining AI Outputs

■ Template:

"Rewrite the following AI-generated response to improve [clarity/conciseness/tone]. Keep the core information intact."

Example:

"Rewrite the following AI-generated response to improve clarity and conciseness. Keep the core information intact."

■ Recursive AI Prompting

■ Template:

"Take this response and refine it by [adding examples/improving readability/making it more engaging]."

Example:

"Take this response and refine it by adding relevant industry examples."

⬤ Bias Mitigation Prompts

■ Template:

"Analyze this AI-generated response for potential bias. Identify any areas where alternative perspectives should be included."

Example:

"Analyze this AI-generated response for potential bias. Identify any areas where alternative perspectives on remote work should be included."

🤖 Technical & Development Prompts

◼ Code Generation

◼ Template:

"Write a [programming language] script that accomplishes [task]. Ensure best practices and code efficiency."

Example:

"Write a Python script that scrapes data from a website and saves it to a CSV file. Ensure best practices and code efficiency."

✗ Code Debugging

◼ Template:

"Here's a piece of code with an error: [insert code]. Identify and fix the issue, then explain what was wrong."

Example:

"Here's a piece of Python code with an error: `print('Hello World)` Identify and fix the issue, then explain what was wrong."

■ API Documentation Writing

■ Template:

"Write clear API documentation for [API functionality]. Include request and response examples."

Example:

"Write clear API documentation for a REST API that retrieves weather data. Include request and response examples."

🔍 Research & Learning Prompts

🍢 Summarizing Complex Topics

■ Template:

"Summarize [topic] in simple terms for a [beginner/intermediate/expert] audience."

Example:

"Summarize quantum computing in simple terms for a beginner audience."

📌 Comparing Concepts

■ Template:

"Compare [concept A] and [concept B]. Highlight key differences and use cases."

Example:

"Compare blockchain and traditional databases. Highlight key differences and use cases."

🤖 AI-Assisted Learning

■ Template:

"Teach me about [topic] using an interactive question-and-answer format."

Example:

"Teach me about machine learning using an interactive question-and-answer format."

🏴 Final Thoughts

Prompt templates **turn AI into a high-performance tool.** Instead of manually crafting every request, use these structured formats to get **faster, higher-quality outputs.**

📌 **How to Use This Cheat Sheet:**
[1] **Modify templates** to fit your needs.
[2] **Experiment**—adjust word choice for better results.
[3] **Stack techniques**—combine structured formatting, role-based prompting, and recursive improvement.

🚀 **Now go build, refine, and let your creativity run free.**

Closing Thoughts: The Future is Prompted – Are You Ready?

You've finally, and truly, reached the end now. So please, indulge me one more time.

This time, I want to leave you with a few thoughts that are purely philosophical.

Is AI a tool? Certainly.

Do I refer to it as a tool? Of course.

But to to call AI *just* a "tool" is to call the symphony a noise, the supernova a spark. Tools chisel stone. This technology we wield transmutes entire landscapes of possibility.

Imagine holding lightning that doesn't only strike, but learns where to carve new rivers. No hammer ever reshaped bedrock by evolving mid-swing. No chisel grew sharper with each fracture it witnessed.

But in truth, although AI can certainly do all of this, what makes the lightning carve those new rivers as well as strike?

Well, the answer is simple. The hands.

The actual limitations of Prompt Engineering and Prompting are mostly the person using it.

Most see a lever. The architect sees a genesis engine.

When intellect compounds—not adds, but multiplies—through recursive loops of silicon and synapse, we breach the event horizon of human capacity.

Tasks dissolve. Problems unravel like threads meeting flame. What emerges isn't automation, but augmentation—a fusion where your mind's outermost edges blur with the machine's boundless terrain. This is true collaboration.

This is no tool anymore but a part of who you are.

All you have to do is witness how X, LinkedIn, Facebook, and other social sites react once ChatGPT goes down or DeepSeek.

You've come this far. You've read the book. You've wandered the labyrinth. Mastered the incantations. Prompting as precise as neural surgery, systems bent to your will like light through prisms.

Yet here, at the precipice, the universe cares nothing for the maps. Only your footsteps.

Although this book is finishing, this moment isn't an ending. It's the beginning.

Will you build shelters with your newfound fire, or forge palaces? The strategist doesn't use. They talk with the so called ghost in the machine, co-authoring realities where yesterday's impossibilities kneel as raw material.

The mountains aren't waiting. They're already moving.

The only choice is whether to stand atop them or perhaps build them yourself.

Because now that you have finished this book? I am certain that dissolving into the sediment beneath, getting left behind, isn't part of your journey.

Now, let's answer some hard truths around AI.

🚀 The Hard Truth About AI Mastery

Most People Will Get AI Wrong

The AI revolution isn't just about DeepSeek, ChatGPT, or whatever you use—it's about how well you **think in AI-first terms.**

Here's the harsh reality:

- **Most people will treat AI like a toy.** They'll ask it trivia questions, use it for generic copywriting, and assume they're "AI literate."
- **Most businesses will underutilize AI.** They'll bolt it onto existing workflows instead of redesigning processes to fully exploit its capabilities.
- **Most professionals will resist AI.** Instead of learning how to use it to multiply their skills, they'll waste energy arguing about whether it will replace them.

🚀 **Your advantage?** You already see AI for what it is: **a thinking machine that can be shaped, directed, and controlled.** You've gone beyond casual use and into **strategic execution.**

Now, the only question is: How will you apply this knowledge?

🏗 The Three Pillars of an AI-Powered Future

To not just survive but **thrive in the AI era,** you need to master three fundamental principles:

1 AI is an Amplifier, Not a Replacement

The best AI users aren't the ones who delegate everything to AI; they're the ones who use AI to **multiply their impact.**

- AI doesn't replace strategic thinking—it **enhances** it.
- AI doesn't replace creativity—it **augments** it.
- AI doesn't replace decision-making—it **provides leverage** to make smarter choices faster.

🚀 What to do now:

- Identify **high-leverage tasks** in your work that AI can amplify.
- Experiment with AI-powered decision support instead of just asking it for information.

- Use AI to generate ideas—but rely on **human insight** to filter and refine them.

---

2 Prompt Engineering is the New Programming

Just like coding once separated technical elites from the rest, **prompt engineering now defines the AI power users.**

AI literacy isn't just knowing how to ask ChatGPT a question. It's knowing:

- How to **structure** prompts for maximum impact.
- How to **debug** AI when outputs are incorrect or weak.
- How to **iterate** prompts to refine and optimize responses.
- How to **stack prompting techniques** (Chain-of-Thought, Recursive Inquiry, Role Assignments, etc.) to extract **higher-order intelligence.**

🚀 What to do now:

- Revisit the **prompt frameworks** in this book and experiment with advanced stacking.
- Treat AI not as a chatbot—but as a **programmable intelligence.**

- Think in **systems**—how can you design workflows where AI handles **execution**, and you handle **strategy**?

---

③ The Winners Will Be the Architects, Not Just the Users

AI is evolving too fast for passive users to keep up. **The people who will dominate this space are those who build AI-powered systems.**

Knowing how to use AI is **step one.** Knowing how to **integrate, automate, and scale AI-driven processes** is the real game.

The highest-leverage individuals in the AI era will be:

- **AI system architects** – People who design workflows that automate entire functions.
- **Prompt engineers & AI trainers** – People who fine-tune AI models and craft expert-level prompts.
- **AI-augmented decision-makers** – Executives, entrepreneurs, and creators who use AI to **compress time, enhance strategy, and build at scale.**

🚀 **What to do now:**

- Move beyond **just using AI**—start **building AI-driven workflows.**
- Learn how to **integrate AI into automation tools** (Zapier, Make, API workflows).
- Train AI models on **your own data** to create **personalized knowledge assistants.**

The future belongs to the builders.

⬤ Your Next Move: Execution Over Theory

You have two choices now:

[1] **Do nothing.** Put this book down and let AI remain a curiosity instead of a competitive advantage.

[2] **Execute ruthlessly.** Apply the principles, refine your prompting skills, and start integrating AI into everything you do.

🚀 Here's a 30-day AI Mastery Plan:

- **Week 1:** Experiment with **advanced prompting techniques** (CoT, recursive, multi-agent).
- **Week 2:** Build an **AI-automated workflow** (content generation, research assistant, data analysis).

- **Week 3:** Join an **AI community** (DeepSeek Discord, Hugging Face forums, Reddit etc) and engage in real-world discussions.
- **Week 4: Optimize and refine.** Test, iterate, and apply AI to a real project or business challenge.

By the end of 30 days, **you won't just be using AI—you'll be operating at a level 99% of people will never reach.**

🚀 Final (Really this time!) Thought: The Future is Prompted—Will You Lead It?

This isn't just another tech wave. **AI is a fundamental shift in how intelligence operates.**

The people who master **AI prompting, automation, and system design** will have **unlimited leverage.**

The people who ignore AI will spend the next decade playing catch-up.

You've just unlocked the playbook. The only thing left to do is execute.

Welcome to the **new era of intelligence.**